YOUR CAREER SANITY:
EARLY EDITION

What the Successful Do Early to Guarantee a View from the Top

C H R I S   M O S E S

NEWMAN SPRINGS PUBLISHING
320 Broad Street
Red Bank, NJ 07701

First originally published by Newman
Springs Publishing 2020

ISBN 978-1-63692-014-6 (Paperback)
ISBN 978-1-63692-215-7 (Hardcover)
ISBN 978-1-63692-015-3 (Digital)

Printed in the United States of America

This book is dedicated to you, the reader, taking an early step to sanely lead your career to high levels

CONTENTS

You'd be stunned if you saw some of the bad actors I've encountered in the workplace. These experiences range from time-wasting employees on Instagram, TikTok, Snapchat, and the like for half the day, to parents calling in angry because I fired their "precious child," to backstabbers and screaming CEOs. It's been a wild ride when I think back on all the "people issues" I've dealt with over the years that I could have avoided if I'd had a road map into my new working world.

When you're new to the workplace, you might not know what it means to be appropriate, to add value, or be the employee that management wants to bump up to the next level. Worse yet, when you make a mistake and do a proverbial face-plant at work, there are typically no mentors to say, "Hey, you made a hot mess out of that one. Next time, try this instead."

I decided it's about time someone put together a simple, easy-to-follow handbook that gives you the rules for *avoiding common workplace blunders, adding the most value, and getting along with others at work*, all of which, coincidentally, are the same as the rules for your best shot at getting ahead.

New and fairly new employees often have crazy ideas about what works, gleaned from reality TV, overpublicized yet uninformative books, or well-meaning friends and family who give you bad advice based on experience they do not have.

How do I know? I screwed up enough times in my early years. Then I finally started getting it right. When I did, I started enjoying work more (most of the time) and definitely moved up the food chain in terms of position, career, and income. It was amazing how quickly I started climbing the ladder of success. I am confident you can do it too.

Let's get started!

CHAPTER 1

YOU GOT THE JOB OFFER—NOW WHAT?

You're excited and ready to go. No longer a cog-in-the-wheel at that last company or a kid at the school that provided that nice leather-bound wall art. It's time to jump out of the nest, fly on your own, and prove to the naysayers in your life that they can enjoy the comfort of your shadow.

Don't expect to have your hand held. Instead, show up ready. Adults don't show up for dinner or a backyard barbeque empty-handed. They bring a bottle of wine or spirits, flowers, or a pie for dessert. Don't show up on day one of your new job empty-handed either. When you arrive sanely ready, it is like starting a 10K foot race at the 6K marker, while all the insane runners are back at the starting line.

Most job offers come by email, so when you get it and you know you want the job, reply with your acceptance within twenty-four hours to show you really want to work at the organization. This is the obvious part of starting your new role. Then do something most candidates have dismissed as a

Boomer action: show a little appreciation and gratitude. The best way to do this is to send a handwritten thank-you note.

You can buy thank-you notes at places like Staples, FedEx Office, or Walmart, and if you are afraid of walking outside, Amazon has hundreds to choose from. You'll need to have the snail mail address for where you'll be working and a stamp so it reaches your new boss. Say something simple like, "Dear Susan: Thank you for selecting me for the financial analyst role. I'm looking forward to working with you, the team, customers, and adding value…" If you don't like this version, there are endless samples on the Internet. Invest a few minutes of research.

You may think a move like this is outdated, but it will be remembered and forever appreciated. In my previous book, *The Sanity Game*, I shared the story of a CEO who writes one hundred thank-you notes every weekend, mostly to employees. He's beloved by all. If he can write one hundred, you can certainly write one.

Sadly, most who send the thank-you note stop there. This is the starting point. If you'll use tools in your role like Word, Excel, or PowerPoint and you are not an expert, spend the time between now and your start date becoming one. Watch YouTube videos and get some fresh training. When you walk in the door, you cannot expect your employer to train you on these things. Take initiative and get ahead of other new hires and current employees. Obviously, you cannot learn everything overnight, so pick up the general concepts and learn a few things really well.

Next, get to know people. You already know who your boss is from your interview. Before showing up on day one, discover the rest of the people in the company. Don't take time interviewing people during your first weeks of employment. Start on LinkedIn, Alignable, Facebook, Twitter,

Instagram, Glassdoor, or other research sites. Get on Google and research. Glean all you can from the company website, review forums, media companies, and earnings reports, and if you happen to have a trusted ally on the inside, obtain as much detail about the work environment as possible. If you're in accounting or any other financial discipline, memorize the financial numbers.

The advantage to all this prework is that you'll become more valuable faster. You'll know the touchstones to strike up a conversation, start building relationships, and work the crowd.

At the end of each chapter are questions to answer. Seriously, answer them. Use code words if you are afraid of others reading your text. Doing this will assist you with figuring out your next step in your own career sanity.

Career Sanity Questions

- What do online articles say about the company's success? How is the company doing financially, and where are they going?
- Who are their customers? What problems do they solve for customers? How does the company make money or acquire donations if they are a nonprofit?
- Who are the important players in the company? What are their names and titles?
- Who will be the people you will be working with on your team? What are their names and roles? Who will you go to if you need help?
- Find out all you can about their interests. Are they passionate about sports? Do they love animals? Do they go to church?

- Is there someone who is steps ahead of you on the same career path that you would like to build a professional relationship with?
- Are you a member of a professional organization related to your industry? (If you are in high school or college, join now and you can get a student discount. It will help you train and be ready. You don't want to show up on day one with nothing to share.)
- Visit Glassdoor to find out about the company. How are they rated regarding salary, training, and benefits?
- Are there professional certifications or licenses you should begin working toward?
- Do you have your "elevator pitch" to describe yourself and your interests to your new colleagues?

CHAPTER 2

WALKING IN ON DAY ONE

It's not about you, it's about them. If you're used to being noticed and receiving constant support and a lot of encouragement, it might be a surprise when you discover that's not how it works in today's fast-paced, information-overload environment. You were hired to add value to the organization, and in the process, you'll want to fit into the environment. Here are the essentials you need to know to have a successful first day at your new job.

Make sure you're dressed appropriately. For starters, be well-groomed and take a shower... *Seriously!*

If you just got a job at Zappos or Google, casual is the name of the game. It's fine to overdress a bit, but don't wear a designer suit. You'll feel out of place, and you'll probably get teased. If you work for Fidelity Investments, that suit might be on point. Never dress to be distracting at work. Consequently, a message T-shirt with a provocative statement or jeans almost ripped to shreds are never a good choice.

When I fly to a company for meetings, I do what I call "corporate stalking." I go near the corporation and walk by. I watch people coming and going. Another idea is to go to a nearby coffee shop where people from the organization might stop. If you discover people are dressed differently from you, it may be wise to make a shopping trip and pick up a couple of items so you look like you belong. A bit of reconnaissance work will give you a good idea what to wear so you fit in, which shows you genuinely want to be there.

On your first day, you're there to absorb value from others. You're not expected to add value yet. So listen. Don't tell them you looked them up online or you'll come across like a stalker. Bring a pad of paper and a pen or pencil. You may need to jot down a few notes. Always have something to write with. And remember your manners. You should ask if the person minds you taking notes.

Be pleasant, warm, and gracious to everyone. This costs zero dollars and becomes a great habit. You certainly don't want to make enemies on your first day. Smile at people and be a little reserved. Don't try to dominate conversations by showing everyone how brilliant you are. Not yet. They'll see that soon enough. For now, focus on listening and learning.

If you're talking with your boss, ask about their goals. You know the goals of the organization because you've researched the company, right? Now is a good time to ask about the goals of your team or department. Ask what your goals should be. Finally, ask your boss and the team how best to communicate. Will your boss want to meet with you daily for three months? Weekly? Or something else? Find out what they consider appropriate, then no one is left wondering.

You'll probably spend time in the Human Resources Department filling out paperwork and setting up your computer. Then your boss will walk you around and introduce you to the people on your team. You should remember their names because you researched them. Joking isn't always wise on your first day until you understand the culture. Humor can be touchy. Right around noon, you'll be taken out to lunch. Finally, you will spend the rest of your day learning what is going on—do not be the first one on the team to go out the door. You can always learn more and let others leave first.

Are you getting a strong sense the place is a loony bin? If your Spidey sense tells you it's an environment where you'll never fit in, it might be a good idea to skip over to chapter 20. Immediately.

Career Sanity Questions

- What should you wear to be dressed right for the environment and culture? This may require you to visit the business location and watch people going to the job. You do not want to show up in a suit if everyone is wearing jeans and vice versa.
- What was on the desks of your new work group? This will provide insight to their personalities and what is important to them.
- Are there a lot of *Dilbert* cartoons on the walls? If so, what are they joking about? This will give an insight to how things are really run at the company. Many *Dilbert* cartoons can be a sign of doom and gloom.
- Do you know how to appropriately shake hands? Do not provide a dead-fish handshake or a bone-crushing one. Make sure you respect the cultures of the employees. Some cultures prefer not to touch.
- How often does your boss want to meet? By the end of the day, have you blocked off the time for the next few months? If you do not have a work com-

puter, put it on your phone calendar. Remember to come prepared to add value at these meetings.

- Have you subscribed to relevant and reputable news sources to receive information relevant to your role and industry? It's probably a good idea to ask your boss what information they prefer to read.

CHAPTER 3

TIME WASTERS AND YOUR CAREER

Now that you've been working a few weeks, you're probably noticing the time wasters coming out of the woodwork. These are people to avoid. Why? Because they take up so much time. They prevent you from adding value in your job by sucking your time away for senseless conversations.

Why do Americans take pride in working so many hours and telling everyone how they toil away for sixty hours a week? It's become a badge of honor, often called the cowboy culture. The truth is, we waste a lot of time. A generation ago, it was known as the "American work ethic" because people really worked hard. Now it's a lie, because so much time is spent on nonproductive activities that don't add value.

How many times do people stop by your workspace to tell you about stuff that doesn't matter, like the details of their kid's birthday party or who's dating whom? This kind of distraction is like a stray cat. Feed it and it'll keep coming back.

I worked at several Fortune 500 companies before starting my company, HR Sanity. To this day, one highly negative person continues saying false things about me. I probably didn't step away from those conversations fast enough. Even worse, those people remember you for those actions and will talk smack about you forever. It becomes a life sentence. Years later, I still watch what I say so nothing gets back to this person. I don't want Medusa's head full of snakes to rise again. You don't want it either.

If you become ensnared in their time-wasting, it will mess up your career. When you get into one of these conversations, get out of it—fast. Say, "Hey, I can't talk right now. I need to get some work done." After a few times, they'll know not to do drive-bys past your workspace. Stop feeding stray cats, and they'll visit a different house for food.

When you don't add value, you limit both your career and income opportunities. Remember, you're not paid to be Mr. or Miss Congeniality—you're paid to get work done. Yes, you can socialize a little; don't be rude. Be aware of how many hours you spend doing what you're paid to do and how many hours you are wasting.

Let's look at the numbers. If you spend one hour a day socializing, that's five hours a week. Multiply it by fifty weeks in a year, and it's 250 hours. That's six and one-quarter weeks of wasted time. Multiply that by two, because socializing takes at least two people.

Everyone needs an outlet to allow their brain time to decompress. Studies say we can work intensely seventy to ninety minutes before we need a break. If you go to the coffee area for a refill and get into a non-value-adding conversation, get out after five minutes. Say, "I have stuff to do. Let's talk more later." You can resume your conversation during lunch.

Avoid the time wasters and find a way to obtain face time with people who can add value to your skills and help you—while you are doing the same for them.

- Who can I learn from?
- Who has the skill sets I want?
- Who adds the most value?
- Who is the best at what they do?

Go to these people when you have a question, so over time you can add more value every day.

Career Sanity Questions

- Who are the time wasters you need to avoid?
- Who are considered the top-performing employees?
- Have you written goals for the next year? If so, find time to discuss the goals with your manager and the top-performing employees.
- What's the latest gossip? If you can answer this question, stop gossiping and focus on adding value.

CHAPTER 4

INTERACTING WITH LEADERSHIP

You may have noticed I write a lot about adding value. When you interact with leaders in your organization, look for ways to make their days or their jobs a little easier. If you're lucky, senior people will like to mentor people, especially younger employees. They enjoy giving valuable advice to help you learn the ropes and avoid landmines.

Go in with a plan, or at least an agenda in your mind, before you talk with them. Understand they're bombarded from multiple angles with people who want to talk to them every day.

Let's do a little more math. If your boss spends thirty minutes a day with six people, that's 180 minutes, or three hours, a day. That's fifteen hours per week just talking. It's fine talking with them to provide an update. Remember in chapter 2, I suggested you ask how they want to receive communication from you? This is where you implement their answer to that question. Don't waste time trying to get to know them or be buddy-buddy with your boss thinking it'll get you to a promotion faster. It usually has the opposite effect. They start believing you're more into trying to be friends rather than your work. Sadly, those people usually end up left behind. Besides, people at work aren't your friends—they're people you work with. Remember, you were hired to add value, not start or join a friend club.

There's no reason you can't communicate with other leaders in addition to your boss. Anyone who is above your level is a leader. Keep in mind the CEO of a Fortune 100 company probably has one or more assistants going through all their communications, so you may not get through to share your great idea.

Let's say you read something in the news relevant to a leader who isn't your boss. Sending or discussing the information is a great way to build the relationship. They begin to know who you are and that you're apprised of the situation and helping to solve problems.

When I talk with leaders, I usually talk in terms of dollar signs, percentages, and graphs. They don't have time for long-winded stories. Don't talk about your daughter's soccer tournament. I guarantee you they're not that interested in your kids. However, they will remember you as a person who's on top of what's going on and knows the data.

If you keep in mind that leaders are only interested in your results and what you're doing to support and add value, you'll keep the conversation focused and dialed in to what matters most to them.

Career Sanity Questions

- At this point, you have been at the job long enough to understand the value you are paid to add. What is that value?
- Can you articulate the value you add in thirty seconds to the levels above you? (Another elevator pitch.)
- Can you articulate the value your team and boss add in thirty seconds?
- What information have you acquired that will help leaders do their jobs better?
- If a leader comes to you with questions about the value you or your team adds, can you answer the question with dollars and percentages? For example, you increased revenue by 15 percent, decreased cost by 10 percent, increased accuracy by 5 percent, yielding x dollars.
- If you have run an analysis on your team and you find that it does not add any value, have you spoken to your boss to make sure you understand your role?

CHAPTER 5

JUNK WORDS TO THROW OUT... *NOW*

So, like, let's be honest here, this chapter clearly, like, exaggerates, like, the, umm, junk words, so, umm, don't get salty—just, like, vibe with the message. I am sure no one reading this will use this level of slang in their lives, but when working with your boss and other leaders, the less slang the better.

Every generation has its own version of slang, but social media, texting, and poop emojis everywhere make for an extreme version of slang. When you don't use adult English, adults think you sound like a teenager. The truth could be that you're working hard and doing your best to add value. Yet when you talk with leaders in your company, they all but pat you on the head and ask if you'd like cookies and milk. If you want to be treated like an adult, talk like an adult and, just as important, write like an adult. Wonder what I'm referring to?

OMG! Like, you know what I mean? Like, it was rad, like, it totally slapped. Like, I was, umm, ya know what I'm sayin'? I literally couldn't believe it, you know? I know, right? Like, seriously? It was Gucci.

Kill the slang. After all, remember, the people you work with are not your close friends. You're not going to Coachella together. Silence is golden and much preferred over talking like you're asking someone to the sophomore dance. When you use slang, you decrease the value of your message.

If you use these words in writing, I'm warning you— your career may hit a brick wall. Wondering why you're still waiting for a job offer? Look over what you're submitting to Monster or Career Builder when you see an interesting job. Does it contain slang? Stop it right now.

Possibly one of the greatest speeches of all time was the "I Have a Dream" speech by Reverend Martin Luther King Jr. But what if he said the words like this?

> "Like, now is the legit time to rise from the dark valley of segregation to the woke path of racial justice. No cap, now is the time to lift our nation from the quick-sand of racial injustice to the lit rock of brotherhood and clap back. I mean, heckin' what, right? It's seriously time to make justice a reality for all God's children and get this bread."

It doesn't sound nearly as impressive and inspiring as the original, does it?

On September 14, 2001, President George W. Bush stood atop the rubble of the 9/11 Twin Towers and said a few stirring words that reassured a frightened nation. But what if he'd grabbed that bullhorn and said,

> "Like, I can hear you, man! I mean, yo peeps! The rest of the world hears you!

The crackheads who literally yeeted these
buildings down will hear all of us soon!"

Can you see and feel the difference from the stirring
originals?

Also, while we're on the subject, it's probably time for you
to nix the smiley faces, pizza slices, thumbs up, poop emojis,
and any other emoji. You're an adult now, remember? These
are sometimes okay as you build personal relationships. But
remember, once the message leaves your phone or computer,
the CEO may see it. Finally, it's probably a good idea to cut
out the nervous laughter and the giggling. Projecting confidence and professionalism will teach others how to treat you.

Career Sanity Questions

- Do you use junk words?
- What junk words do you normally use that you
  need to train yourself not to say? Here is a list to
  get you started: *uhhh, umm, ya know, I mean, dawg,
  like, ya hear me, I said, dude…*
- What junk text do you normally use with work people that you should stop using? Here is a list to get
  you started: LOL, IMHO, AMOF, ROTFLMAO, AYW, CRS,
  WTF… Look at your phone and find the ones you
  need to stop sending to those you work with.
- If the CEO sees your text messages to other
  employees, will it positively or negatively impact
  your career sanity?
- Did you know that if you use a work-provided
  phone, your employer can look at your text messages at any time?

CHAPTER 6

GET TO KNOW THE DATA

Data is essential. In your job, you must know the data because it's the foundation of everything you do at work. You have access to information specific to your role that you must know fluently. When a client company asks me how much salary they're paying annually, I must know that number without even checking. Develop complete command of the data important to you and your customers.

"Trust but verify" is a statement with Russian roots that became famous in the West when President Reagan said it numerous times back in the 1980s. It's become equivalent to a rallying cry when it comes to understanding and evaluating data.

People in the "trust generation" actually trust sources of information on Facebook or Instagram that have no credibility. They even make decisions about how they'll vote based on faulty data. But at work, producing accurate data you can trust is a necessity.

You get to know your own data by paying attention to what you're doing, what your department is doing, and what the company is doing. Use your natural curiosity to ask questions that make sense for you and then look for answers. Here are a few:

- How long does it take you to complete a task? Is that the norm?
- How much time do you spend doing the job you're paid to do?
- In benefits, how much was paid in health insurance premiums?
- In marketing, what is the acquisition cost per customer?
- How many more customers does the company have this year over last year?
- Does increased revenue equate to increased profits?

That's a brief warm-up list of questions. The possibilities are almost unlimited.

People who don't know their own data get stuck doing the same job forever. If you don't know your data, how can people possibly know what value you add?

Become a better analyst by continuing to learn. If you're in accounting, you should already be an excellent analyst. One important tool for you to become proficient in is Microsoft Excel. Lots of YouTube videos can help you gain proficiency with Excel. Or go to a resource like MrExcel.com. Many good books on data analytics can help you understand the fundamentals of data better. Track your personal data at work. How much time are you productive? How much time do you waste?

Knowing important data provides a starting point. Then your job is to continue improving your metrics so you add more value. First, replace the time you spend in the break-room or doing touch-and-gos with more productive activities. These can include time spent working, reading books or articles relevant to what you do, or understanding your industry better. When you know your data, and people know the high level of value you are adding, you'll get paid more, and your career will grow.

Every day you're either accelerating and gaining speed or you're slowing down. There is no "neutral." Remember, your peers and the people around you are doing the same thing. If you don't know your data so you can improve your metrics, you're probably bobbing around in a pond of mediocrity where nothing really changes. Because you're reading this book, I know that's not the future you want.

Career Sanity Questions

- What activities can you measure?
- How can you improve your statistics on these activities?
- Can the measured activities be translated into dollars?
- Will what you do today also improve the metrics of others around you or in a different area?
- Are you at least at an intermediate Microsoft Excel level?

CHAPTER 7

ADD VALUE AND DO IT QUICKLY

I've said it before: when you go to work, it's not about you. The leaders of your organization don't care about your personal binge-watching or the party you went to over the weekend. When you walk in the door, drop everything else in your life for the time that you're there and focus on the value you can add by doing your job efficiently.

When you do that, you'll quickly become respected and appreciated by many. You'll also gather a small group of haters. These are the people who aren't focused on adding value and who mistakenly bring their personal life to work. They'll be left aside as you move forward.

Remember back when you were a teen and it was so important to try to be popular and well-liked? I'm sure you learned over time that you can't make someone like you. It never works. Of course, you're not a robot at work, and you'll have a business relationship with coworkers, people senior to you, and everyone else at work. If you build that relationship around your skills and contributions, you'll be respected for it.

In his book *Results Rule*, author Randy Pennington says, "It's the people in a company that make business work." If everyone at work is laser-focused on results, your organization can become unstoppable and a leader in the industry. Start with you.

When I read Pennington's book, it was like a light came on and the heavens opened. I kept thinking about results, results, results. But I had to add a little sanity to the equation. After all, you're not at work 24-7 and you don't want to tick people off.

I developed a formula called PART. It indicates four components where you emphasize adding value every day:

- *Protect the data.* This is essential in a world where security breaches are an ongoing risk factor.
- *Accuracy.* If your work isn't accurate, you're not adding value.
- *Results.* Get it done.
- *Timeliness.* Do you meet deadlines? How long does it take? Being late and accurate is better than being on time and wrong.

Over the years, most people I've worked with are pleasant, but we're not regularly going out for happy hour together. Make the relationship one based on your contributions. If you're generous about helping them with a work-related question or problem, they'll be happy to return the favor and help you. That's an ideal work relationship.

For clarity, going to happy hour to nurture professional relationships is perfectly acceptable. Remember to be careful with how much you drink and what you say, and do not hug. Hugging will be covered in chapter 16.

Professional relationships are great, but most people you work with aren't your friends. Once you leave the company, you'll probably never talk with most of them again. Real friends are the ones you can borrow money from and never pay back. (I know exceptions to the friend rule. If you have a few long-term friends you met at work, you are fortunate.)

When you come to work with this level of focus every day, you don't waste time on social media or conversations in the breakroom. Yes, you take a break because your brain needs a chance to regroup. When you're thinking, that's work. If you take a walk to clear your head, that's work. You'll accomplish more results in less time because you're not keeping up with Facebook or listening to the details of what happened over the weekend, which wastes your and your organization's valuable time.

Career Sanity Questions

- Where do you focus your value-adding activities? For example, I use PART.
- Is your focus easy to articulate to employees and leaders?
- Are you working on things that should be handled by others?
- When you interact with others, do you come across as a person who performs at a high level or as a person looking for more friends?
- Chapter 1 Career Sanity Questions asked if there was someone who you would like to build a professional relationship with. Have you built relationships with those who can mentor you and provide unvarnished honest feedback?

CHAPTER 8

WHAT'S YOUR JOB?

When you start a new job, you think you know what you'll be doing. I guarantee you'll probably be doing something else. The job description you may receive is a summary of duties, not an all-inclusive training manual.

For example, you might think the job of payroll manager is to make sure payroll is taken care of accurately and on time. A payroll manager actually spends more time handling questions from employees about their pay than anything else.

By about three months in, you generally know what you're doing. As you get to know your role better, you'll probably think of better ways to do it. However, before going to your boss with your brilliant idea, make sure you can articulate it. Even more important is to consider how that change will impact other processes down the line.

For example, you might want to suggest eliminating a field from an important spreadsheet. That might make your job easier, but the information is linked to dozens of other reports throughout the company. It doesn't only affect you—it could have a huge impact on the business. In fact, if a change is made without considering the long-range consequences, it could shut the business down. That would be a stupid move.

Spend your time determining how your idea will impact everyone else so you can champion the path to change. I remember working at a huge company with a paper-based system that was big, ugly, and time-consuming for everyone. It was a hot mess. I thought it would be so much easier if we did it on Excel.

But before making a change, we had to look at the consequences down the line. First, did everyone have Excel? Did they have the right version? How would the data come back? What if people moved to another location within the company?

We discovered half the people didn't have the right version of Excel, and the cost of making the shift for a business with over a thousand stores was $50,000. Ultimately, we decided it was worth the investment because it saved so much time.

Don't shy away from suggesting improvements, but make sure you think things through. Stephen Covey in his best-selling book *The 7 Habits of Highly Effective People* says, "Employers and business leaders need people who can think for themselves—who can take initiative and be the solution to problems." Be a person who takes initiative and is solution-oriented once you know the job you're in.

After a while, you'll probably start thinking about how you can move up. It's impossible to learn how to do the next job up until you fully and completely know the job you have now, just as you must learn basic math before you progress to algebra and then calculus. Everything builds on what you've already learned. After you have your job mastered, start asking for more projects to take on. That's how you learn to be a manager and move up the ladder of success.

Career Sanity Questions

- What is your real job? If it does not match your job description, rewrite the job description.
- What areas of your job do you need some development in? Have you signed up for classes, webinars, or read books on the topic?
- Are you holding on to processes that need to be streamlined because of the old adage "It has always been done this way"?
- Have you written out your processes or created flowcharts to find places to improve?
- If someone asked what you do, could you articulate it in thirty seconds or less? Some experts state that you should be able to articulate in it six seconds. Try that one.

---— CHAPTER 9 ——●

YOUR ATTITUDE IMPACTS YOUR SUCCESS

It's simple: people don't want to be around a grouch all day. I see a lot of people who bring their personal crap into the workplace, whether it's their heartache, unpaid bills, political views, or the cat who keeps throwing up on the sofa. Trust me, no one really cares. Bringing it to work creates a negative environment, which reduces productivity for you and everyone.

The world outside your job could be falling apart with family problems, swarms of locusts, or a pandemic. Choose to keep your distance from those things while you're at work. You have a job to do. Get to work and focus on adding value.

Cy Wakeman, author of *Reality-Based Leadership*, says, "Whether you believe something possible or impossible— either way, you will be right."

When people say I can't do something, I love it when I prove them wrong. Believe the world provides almost unlimited possibility, and that mindset will increase your confidence. Be positive about yourself and ignore the endless turmoil and utter hopelessness you see hour after hour on the news. When you choose to feel more confident, you'll try more things, and you'll be more likely to succeed. Plus, with your can-do attitude, more and more people will want to be around you.

When I started HR Sanity, almost everyone I know said, "Chris, what are you doing? You have to get a job!"

I replied, "You work at a corporation, and someone started it. Someone had the nerve to walk away from their job and strike out on their own." I'm pleased to say since I started my business in April of 2017, I've had many ups and downs—luckily, more ups than downs. When people think you can't do it and you do it anyway and prove them wrong, it's a blast, as long as it is legal and adds value.

Whenever someone says, "No, Chris, it's a bad idea," I like to dig deeper and ask questions like, "I wonder why they're saying that? Is it because of a personal bias? Maybe they don't want to work and would rather watch Netflix and chill?" You'd be amazed how many people don't want to work and go the extra mile.

For me, that mindset probably sprang from growing up as a poor kid in a poor town. Growing up in poverty was a great motivator for me. If you didn't grow up wanting the simple things, find your motivation by looking to people who are successful. Many millionaires and billionaires didn't have it handed to them. They started something. Look to successful people who have what you want.

Fred Smith received a C+ on a paper for a business class about a personal delivery service. Years later, the idea turned into his company, Federal Express.

Eileen Collins had a dream to be an astronaut. Everyone told her it was impossible. A woman couldn't do it. But she followed a path and refused to listen to the naysayers. In 1991, she became an astronaut. In 1995, she was the first woman to pilot the space shuttle. No one was going to tell Collins no.

I stay positive by looking at people's negative stuff and decide I don't want to be that. They're idiots. I am grateful for what I do have but also happy I'm not a negative, complaining jerk. Negativity drags everyone down. Whatever it takes for you to ignore the negative, focus on what you have and what you can improve.

Career Sanity Questions

- What drama are you bringing to work each day? Stop doing it! It does not matter to your team.
- What negative "can't do" items can you fix for others? For yourself?
- Who are the negative people to avoid?
- What are some of the things you were told as a child you could not do that you now have the opportunity to prove everyone wrong about and enjoy the success? For me, it was world travel. Because of hard work, I have traveled to dozens of countries.

CHAPTER 10

YOU'RE NOT THE CEO—NOT YET

"See this whiteboard," my boss said. He was an executive vice president, perched many levels above me, known to all as a genius in his field. For clarity, he really was a genius in the field. I nodded. I was young and thought I was full of great ideas, ready to change the world. I wanted to move up fast.

He took a marker, drew a chart, and put a little dot at the bottom. "This is you," he continued. Then he put a big dot at the top of the chart and said, "This is me." He paused for emphasis. "Me. You," he said pointing to the respective dots. Finally, "You do your job down here, and I'll do my job up here."

I was embarrassed. I walked back to my cubicle and sank into my chair, flushed with anger. But after time passed, I realized he was right. I never forgot that lesson.

You're young or early in your career and learning the ropes. You may think you have a great idea that'll make executives sit up and take notice. Maybe you do have a game changer. However, at this early stage, you don't understand the impact your idea could have on marketing, distribution, operations, and every other facet of the business. Remember, the reason your boss turned down your terrific idea isn't necessarily because he or she doesn't like you. It's entirely possible it is a good idea, just not right now. Believe me, if they think it's a dumb idea, they'll probably let you know.

So go ahead and express your idea, but don't get upset when it can't be done.

A few years later, I came up with an idea that would solve a lot of problems at the $3 billion company where I worked. The idea cost only $5 million. It was a drop in the bucket for such a huge company.

However, I didn't understand the whole story. They were trying to buy a $6 billion company. In the short term, they needed to protect and preserve all the cash they could. The timing wasn't right. But at the time, I didn't know these top-level secrets, and you won't know them either. Leadership has a better understanding of the bigger picture.

While your idea might impact a lot of other areas of the company, it might not fit in with the long-term strategy. The timing may be off, or it may not be a priority. There can be a multitude of reasons why a new idea isn't adopted.

How many big projects do you think were canceled because of the 2020 COVID-19 crisis? Upgrading systems, buying companies, investing in employees, designing new products, and many other services were put on hold or canceled.

Keep doing your job. Keep learning and training. But don't take it personally, and don't give up on it either. If your boss turns down an idea but says, "Maybe later," ask him or her when you should bring it up again.

Ask, "Can we revisit it in another three months or six months?" Find out when "later" is and schedule a time to take a deeper dive later.

Even if your idea can't be implemented now, your boss will appreciate the fact that you're thinking. He will remember the fact that you want to add value and make things better for the company and for everyone.

Career Sanity Questions

- What are the big ideas that may be a game changer for your organization?
- Can you articulate these game-changing ideas?
- Do you have the value broken down into dollars and percentages?
- What is the cost of these game-changing ideas?
- How can you bring these to your boss's attention without overstepping his/her role in the organization? Note: going above your boss with game-changing ideas is a really, really, really, bad idea. Jumping to the CEO without following the chain of command is a sure way to get blacklisted.

CHAPTER 11

HAVE A TRAINING PLAN

My grandfather used to say, "When someone else pays for something, it's always a bargain." So when the company you work for provides training, take advantage of it. No one is going to hold your hand and walk you through it. You're responsible for taking the initiative to professionally and personally develop yourself. If it's offered, take it. If you were raised with helicopter parents, it's time to toughen up a bit and be the captain of your own ship. Take the right actions to improve your skills and keep striving to become a better version of you.

If you just left college, you may think you're trained and ready, but you're not. You were hired for your skills and ability to learn. You were also hired for your potential. However, if you don't do anything with that potential, it's wasted. Don't be resentful of the fact that you need more training. An attitude of "I don't want to do any more than I have to" isn't going to help you move up and succeed and won't help you better yourself.

The great news about training is that most professional and personal development is provided online. Each module you complete will take only a few minutes and teach you things in minutes that could take you years to learn on your own. Working on a training plan shows your boss that you're on top of things and being responsible about your career. Plus, it will put you in line for a promotion sooner. There's no good reason you can't put at least thirty minutes of your time each week into training.

During personal time, everyone needs a mental break to get away from the stresses of life. I am not saying that watching a few episodes of your favorite show is a bad idea. The message is to spend a little less personal time with the shows and more time on your development.

Outside your organization, there's an endless array of training available for free. A woman I've worked with told me she trained herself as a teen to have good etiquette. She figured if she's ever invited to the White House for a state dinner, she'll feel comfortable about which fork to use rather than stabbing her food. She's never attended a state dinner, but she's had dinner with CEOs a few times and feels self-assured and comfortable in that environment because of her training.

Excellent training is available online for little or no cost. Check out Khan Academy, Coursera, and *The Great Courses.* There's even free training offered through Harvard and Yale. Think about where you want to go in your career. Maybe you want to take an international assignment. You can learn a new language over time with Rosetta Stone. Your library may even offer it for free.

If the thrill is gone in your job, get more training and prepare yourself for a new position that's more in alignment with your interests.

Never turn down free training. Create a goal to continue becoming better and better, growing in the direction of your greatest goals.

Career Sanity Questions

- What is your professional training plan for the next week, month, quarter, year, decade?
- Have you blocked time to work on your training plan?
- Are there coworkers who would benefit by training with you?
- Can you train others on one of your skills?
- Are you saving a little each paycheck to pay for training that your employer will not cover?

CHAPTER 12

PROFESSIONAL ORGANIZATIONS

It's not only important to become known on your team, in your department, and in your organization. It's also important to become known within your industry. Becoming a member of a professional organization within your field is a great way to do that.

Professional organizations exist to support people in many professions and trades. They provide three primary benefits to their members:

- Great networking opportunities with people in your profession.
- Career development and self-paced learning.
- Membership that will look great on your resume (a leadership role will look better).

When you join a professional organization, you'll find many opportunities to volunteer. Talk to the board about what you can provide to other members or the community. Some people will teach a class. I've taken on the task of calling all the people who need to renew their memberships in my organization each month. I get to talk with forty people a month and ask them to renew their membership, but who knows what else could come out of those conversations?

Once you've volunteered successfully for a while, look for an opportunity to serve on the board. Stick with it, and you can become vice president or president of your local chapter. This will look even better on your resume.

One important caution about volunteering: the idea is for volunteer activities to enhance your job, not to get in the way of your job. Once they see you follow through and do what you said you'll do, they'll start coming to you with more volunteer activities. It's way too easy to get roped into things. If you have the time, do it. If you don't, it's better to politely decline.

If you look at the demands of your job and your personal life and it simply isn't realistic to take on any more, say something gracious like, "Thank you very much for the offer. I wish I could. I just can't put any more on my plate right now."

When you're seen as that can-do person who gets things done, your brand or reputation within the organization will soar. On the flip side, if you say you're going to volunteer, and you don't follow through with what you said you'd do, you lose trust and credibility within the organization and across your industry.

If you're still in school or you've recently graduated, they probably have a student rate for membership which will make joining and participating more affordable for you.

Finally, professional organizations often have great publications. Usually they're accessible online. These e-magazines or publications are a helpful source of learning and training, so you become more skilled and gain the opportunities to move up in your career.

Career Sanity Questions

- What are the professional organizations you could join?
- If your employer will not pay for the membership, are you willing to invest in yourself?
- If you do not have the funds to join the professional organization, are there others on your team you could partner with and share a membership or borrow material?
- What volunteer opportunities provide the most value to you and don't inconveniently take time from your employer?

CHAPTER 13

STANDING ON A SOAPBOX: A RECIPE FOR DISASTER

"But you don't know what I'm going through!" my coaching client whined. He was embroiled in a divorce and mentioned talking with a coworker about his marital troubles.

"How many people are you talking about this with at work?" I asked.

"Oh, maybe a dozen," he replied.

I shook my head in dismay. "Why are you doing that? Don't do that. They're not your friends. They're not your therapist or your bartender either," I reminded him.

When you whine and moan about personal problems at work, it destroys your promotability.

Standing on a soapbox falls into two categories:

- Griping and moaning about the personal struggles in your life.
- Complaining and pointing out everything wrong about where you work.

As a new employee at your company, you probably don't have a good understanding of the way things work yet. You might think it's okay to treat your coworkers like you did with your college buddies sitting around eating pizza and drinking beer. Don't be a complainer or a whiner. Your coworkers and leadership have no loyalty to you. They might be polite and smile, but that doesn't mean they agree. Keep in mind when you no longer work there, you'll probably never talk with your coworkers again. Making a name for yourself as a person who constantly finds fault is a recipe for disaster. It will slowly destroy your career.

It might seem strategic to try and build alliances by loudly pointing out what you believe is wrong about the company. In the process, you make your boss, the CEO, and the company look bad. When you talk smack, it reflects negatively on the whole team, and, worst of all, it reflects poorly on you as a potential leader as well as a person.

Don't say or do anything to threaten your boss, even if you can't stand him or her. It's far easier to get the boss promoted by adding more value and talking them up rather than tearing them down. When you try to hurt your boss or others by saying negative things, word will get back to them that you're bad-mouthing others behind their back. Your job could end up on the chopping block. So draw a line in the sand and stop it.

Instead, figure out how to make your boss look good. After all, you're partners, like Batman and Robin. Whatever you're working on goes into your boss's hands. It's the company's work product, not yours, so give it your best. Have solutions to the problems you're all dealing with together. Look for what you can say that's positive and focus more on learning and listening.

If you want to have friendly breakroom conversations, talk about the weather, sports, or things happening in your community or around the world. Talk about "outer things" happening rather than highly personal or opinionated "inner things."

In my book *The Sanity Game*, I wrote, "The truth will set you free—but first it will piss you off." If you're feeling a little ticked right now, I bet you've been doing some of your own conniving at work. Stop it immediately. Then gradually let people see a more positive, value-adding, solution-oriented you.

Career Sanity Questions

- One question only for this chapter: do you preach from your soapbox? If so, *stop it!*

CHAPTER 14 ──●

HOW TO GET PROMOTED: THE UNWRITTEN TRUTH

You want to know how to get promoted, right? Add more value than others around you. You've already read "add more value" in this book several times, but what does it mean when you want to move up in the company?

Start by becoming very good at your job. In fact, get close to mastering it. Then begin preparing for your next role.

You've identified a need within your area because you're paying attention. You want the chance to go ahead and solve the problem or change the world with your own team. Ask your boss if you can take on a project you can manage or lead with a team. You're already adding tons of value in the job you've mastered, so they're not worried you might fall behind in your primary job.

Start developing a personal brand as a low-drama person who gets things done. You're slowly getting seen by your coworkers and leadership as a person who is accurate, who does things right, and who's solution oriented.

Don't play office politics at work. It's playing with fire. But the politics matter. Do your best to get along with everyone. This will put you on the map because you're different from so many other people. Leadership will start noticing you, and before you know it, you'll be in the thick of things.

Will there be haters? Probably, as there always are. When you find them, smile. Having haters is a sign that you are doing something right. People who are jealous or resentful are always trying to pull down winners who add value like the proverbial crab in the bucket. Don't let them get to you. Keep treating everyone you come in contact with respectfully. If they talk behind your back but everyone else sees you as amazing, they'll become known as the whiny complainer you will never be.

As a person who does great work, is solution oriented, and doesn't get in the weeds of office politics, you'll develop a brand as a promising person with a great future. Your brand doesn't happen overnight, but once you create it, it will follow you around forever. Some people might call it your reputation. Do the right things for years, and you'll have a solid brand at work as a winner.

What do you become known for? When people hear your name, they'll think of a friendly, low-drama person who solves problems, knows how to lead a team, and who gets things done and gets them done right. That will set you up for a promotion.

Career Sanity Questions

- Are you fully proficient in your current role?
- How's that training plan? Does it include training for the next level in your career path?

- As things become difficult and stressful, are you looked upon as someone who can stay levelheaded?
- Who are the haters you need to stay away from?

CHAPTER 15

PEOPLE WHO MAKE YOUR LIFE HELL

Some people you work with will haunt you wherever you go. They may be monsters right from the get-go, or perhaps you were rude to them once, and they will never let you forget. It could be years since you left the company where you first encountered them, but they'll still bad-mouth you every chance they get.

Yes, you're forced to work with them. You don't have much of a choice. So give them what they need: be polite and avoid them like a plague.

Years ago, I worked with a person who simply wasn't a good leader. She did everything possible to make other people look bad with the misguided idea it would make her look good. These people are sneaky. They do their dirty work behind your back and smile to your face. This person seemed to get pleasure from hurting good people and their careers. Ten years later, long after I'd left the company and started my own business, she's still lying and telling people what a horrible person I am.

Many of these terrible people will become threatened if they start thinking you're smarter than them. Eventually, you'll be fired for knowing more than they know. Get away as fast as you can.

These types of people and companies treat employees like crap. Then they're surprised when good people go running for the doors. They're forever saying bad things that are mostly untrue.

Don't spend time with people who make your life hell. If you see them treating other people horribly and they're nice to you, don't think you miraculously dodged a bullet. It's a temporary state. Eventually they'll make their way to you, and your head will be the one on the chopping block.

In the working world, if someone bad-mouths others to you, they're also bad-mouthing you to others. Avoid these two-faced demons.

My daughter was once upset about someone at school who didn't like her. Despite her attempts, she still couldn't make a friend of this one person in her class.

I asked her, "Honey, if you pet a dog and it bites you, would you pet it again?"

"Well, maybe once," she replied.

"That's right." I explained to her, "Some people are just mean and awful. It doesn't mean you're not a wonderful person. You can't change them. So don't pet the dog that bites you. Just keep your distance."

Career Sanity Questions

- Are there people in your environment who can make your life a living hell?
- Can you avoid these people?
- Can you limit the amount of time spent with them?
- What can you do to ease their anger toward you?
- Are you ready to jump ship? If so, skip ahead to chapter 20.

CHAPTER 16

IT STARTS WITH A HUG

Let's start with a myth. Boys will be boys, and girls will be girls. Nope, not true. People will be who they want to be; they will not be forced into stereotypes. More importantly, the entire workforce must act with respect and honor everyone's uniqueness. To do this correctly, you must be vigilant with your words and personal space.

Here is the ridiculousness of human behavior. As teenagers, some friends encourage us to act out and tell bad jokes. As we grow up, it becomes part of our personal brand, and we're sometimes trying to outdo each other and tell the most awful jokes. On the other end of the spectrum, there are people who were raised to be people pleasers and discouraged from communicating directly when something makes them uncomfortable.

Regardless of the hints you think coworkers are dropping in the workplace or how well you think you understand their senses of humor and boundaries, it is not acceptable to flirt at work, touch someone, or make comments on race, religion, or sexual orientation. When this occurs, the offender is participating in harassment.

Don't get caught up in the popular "That's what she said" line. It gives bad jokes, inappropriate behavior, and sexual references a stamp of approval. If you let it go, it's almost guaranteed another person will raise the bar and tell a joke that's even worse. People do it because they want to be seen as cool and be accepted. Coworkers sometimes giggle with nervous laughter at the jokes because they don't want to be labeled as a prude or a tattletale. Even if a coworker genuinely thought the joke was funny or perhaps made the joke themselves, that doesn't mean it's appropriate behavior at work.

If it's inappropriate—stop it. Remember, you're not being paid to tell stupid or sexual jokes. You're not being paid to find your mate or spouse either. If someone calls you out on it, do not fight; instead, take some time to reflect. An apology may be needed.

It's natural to try to get the crowd laughing, but not all jokes are for work or coworkers, and laughter and joking can easily lead to even more inappropriate behavior. Then the touching starts—a forearm, a shoulder. It's all innocent enough. A hug is the gateway, then there's a longer hug. Next, there's a kiss on the cheek. Before you know it, you're going out for cocktails or to dinner. Then you're getting a hotel room.

So cut out any touching and especially the hug. I have a no-hug policy at work because I don't want to give the impression I'm opening the door to more. I also don't tell sexual jokes.

Remember, many harassment claims start with joking. Years later, it can result in a lifetime of pain as someone remembers your behavior from a long time ago and tells everyone.

If the jokes are going overboard and you believe they are getting to the point of harassment, try this before you talk with your Human Resources Department. Send a detailed email to the person, or group, who is making your life difficult with inappropriate behavior. Document in detail

1. What they did;
2. how it made you feel; and
3. what behavior you expect from them going forward.

Before hitting the send button, carefully reread your e-mail. The person may share the e-mail, and you want to make sure the facts are stated clearly and concisely.

Studies have shown an e-mail like this can have a positive result. Don't be offensive or combative. State the facts from your vantage point. They'll finally wake up and understand how their behavior impacts you. Also, they'll notice you're documenting what's happening, and they'll know you could go to the Human Resources Department with it.

Clearly, if there is inappropriate behavior going on beyond the annoyance of stupid jokes, or if you feel threatened, go to the Human Resources Department. They are there to protect you and the company.

Remember this kind of bad behavior can follow you around for decades. When you are in a position of authority and have risen the ladder of success, you'll be remembered for how you acted back then. Being remembered as honorable is much better than the alternative.

Career Sanity Questions

- Does the organization's culture encourage harassment? If so, go to chapter 20.
- Are the jokes you tell okay for a child to hear?

- Did you know that harassment comes in all forms? Be careful not to be the perpetrator.
- Are you a hugger? If you are...*stop!*

CHAPTER 17

SHARING YOUR CREATIVE IDEAS

There is glory in being the person who has the great idea that will change how business is done, introduce a new product, or save the world from global warming. However, chances are that the idea has already been tried and failed. That is why when you come up with these great ideas and share them with your boss, they are shot down. The only words you remember during your moment of anger is your boss saying, "It's not going to work."

Ugg those Boomers!

The reality is that many ideas have been tried, and something unanticipated brought the idea to a screeching halt. Your idea may have been shot down but it is not dead yet. It may need a few adjustments and a fair amount of collaboration to engage the naysayer at a different level.

To share your ideas and receive better results, be faithful to the facts and engage many coworkers. You probably do not have all the facts—generally, no one does. By engaging multiple coworkers from different disciplines, you will understand a bigger picture of your idea's impact and build a support team. There might be a lot of lively discussion back and forth as people bounce ideas around; the original idea morphs and changes until it's finally ready.

Taking a few lessons from others will provide additional guidance on how to share your creative ideas. Here are a few:

1.   Stephen Covey: "Start with the end in mind."
2.   Shepard Fairey: "Creating is about sharing ideas, sharing aesthetics, sharing what you believe in with other people."
3.   Oliver Wendell Holmes: "Many ideas grow better when transplanted into another mind than into the one where they sprang up."

As you follow these three points, the business-changing idea you present will not be the same as when you first thought of it. It will be stronger, more impactful, supported by many, and much easier to communicate to your boss or other leaders.

Thomas Edison coined my favorite quote for creating new concepts: "I learned ten thousand ways not to make a light bulb." This is what your idea may be like. Many tries, many misses, many conversations—then you will figure out how to change the world.

Career Sanity Questions

•   Why did your idea not work last time? This time?

- Who are the people in your network who will provide feedback that will make your ideas and concepts better?
- How can you fix the faults of your ideas?
- Are you upset by the feedback? If so, stop being upset. Feedback is the breakfast of champions!

CHAPTER 18

HOW *NOT* TO GET PROMOTED

The first seventeen chapters have provided multiple methods to add value and get promoted. Doing the exact opposite is an easy way to receive a one-way ticket out the door or a way to enjoy your assigned seat for years to come.

By far the easiest way to keep the same role for years and never receive a promotion is to talk negatively about your boss, anyone at or above your boss's level, or customers. Leaders notice who is spitting venom.

Even worse is talking negatively about your boss in hopes to get the boss fired so you can move into their role. I have seen this multiple times and can 100 percent guarantee that this technique will not work. This will blow up in your face.

Let's say you are successful getting your boss fired. You have a reputation of trashing bosses to get ahead, so why would they want to promote you?

There are much better ways to get promoted. For starters, try to help your boss get promoted. When you do this, your relationship with your boss will be much better, other leaders will notice how you added value to your boss, and now your boss's role needs to be filled with someone who will make your boss's former boss look good. Ta-da! That person is now you.

Sometimes, things will not be going well between you, your coworkers, your boss, or others in leadership. The first thing most people do is to discuss these issues with others, generally making the other person look bad. This is commonly called backstabbing.

Most of the time, you will not have the full story, or at least you won't know what is going through the other person's mind. In chapter 10, I discussed a time when I did not know the entire story. Thankfully, I used a much better approach to handle the situation. This approach is called "stabbing from the front."

It is easy to bad-mouth someone to others. A person who wants to get promoted needs to become comfortable taking their issues to the source. When you talk in front of the person, you are stabbing from the front. It is not the most comfortable thing to do, as the person you are talking to may be the problem.

Even though there may be friction during the stabbing from the front conversation—for instance, you may be upset after they share their truth about the situation and find that you were completely wrong with your assessment—you will be better off and be looked at as a partner. Most leaders and coworkers want others in their circle they can trust. They want the type of person who will directly discuss disagreements and work toward a shared solution. Backstabbing never fixes issues. Front-stabbing builds trust and gets you in line for more responsibility.

Career Sanity Questions

- Did you know once you say to someone, "I want your opinion of this person, and it needs to stay between us," the detail rarely stays "between us"? This is why backstabbing fails.
- If you believe there is a better way to do something your boss has asked you to do, have you brought this up to your boss? If you are worried, try this statement, "(Boss), I do not believe in going behind people's backs when I disagree. This is backstabbing. I would like to try a little stabbing from the front to tell you why this can be done better…" They may laugh at first then listen.
- How are you preparing your boss for their next role?

CHAPTER 19

THE WORLD OF WRITE-UPS

In all my corporate years before starting my own business, I was never written up. I did plenty of dumb things, but here's the truth: managers and bosses hate writing people up. It's one of the worst things they have to do. Can you imagine having to take time to write something honest, articulate, and in such a way the company won't be sued? I hated having to write people up. If you have been written up, chances are you did something so stupid you deserved it. Reflect on it, make changes, and don't take what you did to your next job.

Then again, it might not be the end of the world. Being written up happens outside your annual review. They usually say, "We're putting this in your permanent file." You'll probably get a verbal warning first. When you're written up, it's usually not a surprise.

Some write-ups are easily fixable. For example, if you get written up because you come in fifteen minutes tardy every day, you can get your butt out of bed earlier and get to work on time. Performance mistakes that upset the team and the company are a different matter. Fix them by spending an extra ten minutes making sure your work is done right before submitting it. If time permits, take a longer break between completion and submission to allow you time to think differently about the product. I think almost everything is fixable. However, if the problem is a cultural one, make sure to read chapter 20.

Being written up might be a sign it's time to start looking for your next job. A write-up isn't a brick wall yet, but they've started building that wall. You can still jump over it.

Being written up can kill your promotability, which means you probably won't move up as quickly, and you'll receive fewer or smaller pay raises. The key is to learn from your mistakes and improve the behavior. It's a clear opportunity to fix what isn't working and rebuild trust so you rebuild a negative brand into a positive one.

One guy who was written up reflected on his problems and figured out how to fix them. He started getting noticed for the right things, moved up, and became a top executive. Being made aware of the problems helped him.

Occasionally a boss just plain doesn't like someone and will write them up because they have it in for them. You might not be fitting into the culture of the company. You might be breaking rules, even unwritten ones. Break big rules, and you may not be able to ever get back into their good graces.

Sometimes employees will say, "I'm not signing that." It still goes in your folder. It's petty and makes a person who's written up look even more argumentative.

To confuse the person who writes you up, smile and say, "Thanks for the feedback." Most people leave a write-up meeting acting mad or grumpy. Saying "Thanks for the feedback" moves you away from the problem faster. It says you listened and accepted the feedback. It doesn't necessarily say you agree with them.

If you decide it's time to move jobs, you will start fresh. Write-ups don't move with you to your next company, and there's nothing wrong with that. Learn from the experience, fix the problems, and unless you're passionate about the company, think seriously about moving elsewhere.

Career Sanity Questions

- Are you anticipating a write-up soon? If so, have you reflected on how you have not added value? Can it be fixed? Is this a culture issue?
- What behaviors and value-added results can you adjust before (or after) the write-up?
- Have you implemented any of the previous chapters? Seriously? If you are written up because you are adding value and helping others, the time to leave is now. Go to the next chapter.

CHAPTER 20

WHAT IF IT DOESN'T WORK?

The answer is simple. Go underground and find a new job. Why do I say, "Go underground?" Because if your company isn't happy with you, your boss is probably already out there looking for your replacement. It's not a good idea for him or her to find you online tossing out resumes like you're scattering buckshot.

Don't look for new jobs on your company computer where you can be discovered. Use your personal phone during break times. You should be a little bit covert about this operation. Go to a site like UpWork.com to hire a virtual assistant for $5 to $10 USD per hour. They can comb different websites looking for leads for you so you can follow up on the ones that interest you.

There are many different sites for job hunting based on the industry you're in. The best sites for business are Indeed and LinkedIn. Indeed.com scrapes many sites and puts the job listings in one location. Recruiters go to LinkedIn.com because it has the best tools for recruiters. Sites like Monster and CareerBuilder are yesterday's news.

Getting out the door as fast as possible isn't necessarily what you want. Someone once told me, don't quit one job before you get the next one lined up. Why? Because there's no honor in being broke and begging for money. To preserve self-respect, don't go back to Mom and Dad. Do you really want to be treated like a kid again and have to follow their house rules? Once you're an adult and out of their house, you're out for good.

Maybe your last job wasn't in the right field for you. Find something that fits you. If you're a night owl, you don't want to have to start making the donuts at 4:00 a.m. I have a friend who works the midnight shift at UPS, and it's perfect for her. She makes great money, all her bills are paid, and she has a life that's right for her.

If you're looking, do whatever you can offline by talking with recruiters. Have them look over your resume. Connect with people you've met who might provide helpful tips and are willing to share their experience and knowledge.

In my previous book, *The Sanity Game*, I wrote that many jobs have lousy job descriptions that are highly inaccurate. Finding the truth can take some detective work. My best suggestion is to look at Glassdoor.com to see what's really going on with a company. Call people up with the job you might apply for to find out what's really happening. You can simply make up a name for yourself if you want to keep things covert.

By the way, when it comes to adding value, this isn't a time to slow down before you say, "So long!" Add even more value now. Don't leave on bad terms and end up with a life sentence. It will come back to bite you later. Do everything possible to make your boss look good before you take off. Then they'll regret that you left, and you'll walk out that door for the very last time with your head held high on the most positive note you possibly can.

Career Sanity Questions

- Many leave their first few jobs because of the organization or their culture, only to have the same struggles at future jobs. Are you sure that the issues are not self-inflicted?
- Have you checked the Glassdoor.com ratings of the potential future organizations? Do not put much trust in the five-star ratings, because some companies encourage employees to inflate the score. Focus more on the one-star through three-star ratings to obtain a clearer picture of what you may be walking into.
- Have you spent any time mending ties with the coworkers you have butted heads with? They may become the next CEO. A statement that has worked for me is: "Hey <name>, wanted to let you know that I am leaving the organization. I know we did not agree on everything and even butted heads a few times. While these may have been negative situations, they allowed me to think differently and grow after the encounter. Thank you for helping me during all of those encounters." Best if said in person.

CONCLUSION

This book should have provided you with the strategies you need to be recognized as a valuable employee your company won't want to let go. When they see you as the kind of person who has a bright future with the company because you excel at your role, you add more value, and you know how to get along to keep things moving smoothly.

I learned through trial and error what it's like to botch things up and how it feels when you start getting things right. Believe me, life is much better when things are right.

As crazy as our world is today with lightning-fast changes in technology and culture, some things don't change a whole lot at work. These rules for being a winner and the kind of employee everyone likes having around are at the top of the list.

Now that you know the rules of *Your Career Sanity* as I've shared them, I wish you smooth sailing and much success as you strive to incorporate them into your life and your career.

ACKNOWLEDGEMENTS

A large debt of gratitude goes to all the leaders during my early career insanity. Without them, finding sanity would have never been possible. Fortunately, these early leaders spent more time laughing at my theories of work than crushing my ambitions. In order of tax paying jobs, Mike, Coleman, Bryan, Laurie, Curt, Rich, another Rich, Eileen, and Susan, thank you for creating a positive impression that has been added to the book. And, thank you to the early leaders who have hired HR Sanity to help maintain their organization's sanity.

Let me acknowledge you, the reader, for reading the acknowledgements. You have come this far in the book and continued reading. Maybe the time has come for you to acknowledge those in your life, who have provided guidance on your journey. Remember in chapter 1, "You can buy thank-you notes…"

Send those you would like to acknowledge a thank-you note, even if you haven't talked to them in many years.

Finally, a big thank you to the dozens of people who helped review the book, DFWWC editors, and the restaurant, TruFire Kitchen, in Southlake, Texas, who let me have four hour lunches to write parts of the book in the corner of the building.

ABOUT THE AUTHOR

Chris Moses is an engaging professional who has spent more than twenty years adding value to companies ranging from small one-person businesses to Walmart. His coaching clients consist of professionals ranging from entry level to CEOs. He follows the one-size-fits-one philosophy to increase top and bottom lines, provide career guidance, and consult with global organizations.

Ready to increase the value of your company, non-profit, or school by sharing Your Career Sanity?

Changing from a level of insanity to sanity is not easily done alone. When you are ready to introduce your groups to *Your Career Sanity*, Chris's team at HR Sanity is available to assist. Chris challenges audiences to take a deep look into their environment and take responsibility for the needed changes. His approach is direct, based on the facts, adds a little finesse, and is fun. Through engagement, relationships improve, teams become dynamic, attitudes change, and both sanity and value are added to every aspect of participants' lives. Everyone leaves with an actionable plan to create sanity for themselves and their organization.

Ready to take the next step? Contact Chris directly at chris.moses@HRSanity.com or call the sanity hotline at +1-833-4-SANITY (1-833-472-6489).